once

contents

ISBN 978-1-4768-1371-4

HAL•LEONARD®
CORPORATION
7777 W. BLUEMOUND RD. P.O. BOX 13819 MILWAUKEE, WI 53213

In Australia Contact:
Hal Leonard Australia Pty. Ltd.
4 Lentara Court
Cheltenham, Victoria, 3192 Australia
Email: ausadmin@halleonard.com.au

Visit Hal Leonard Online at
www.halleonard.com

FALLING SLOWLY

Words and Music by GLEN HANSARD
and MARKETA IRGLOVA

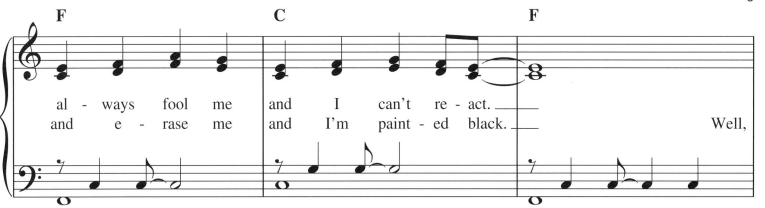

al - ways fool me and I can't re - act.
and e - rase me and I'm paint - ed black. Well,

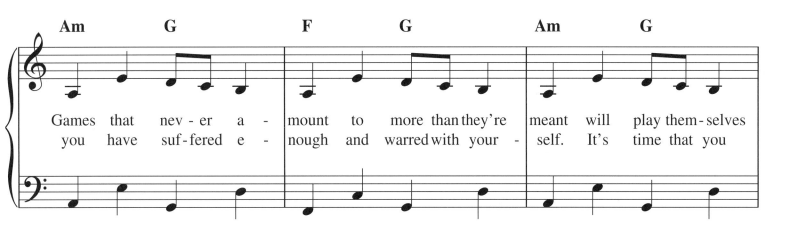

Games that nev - er a - mount to more than they're meant will play them - selves
you have suf - fered e - nough and warred with your - self. It's time that you

out.
won.

cresc.

Take this sink - in'
mf

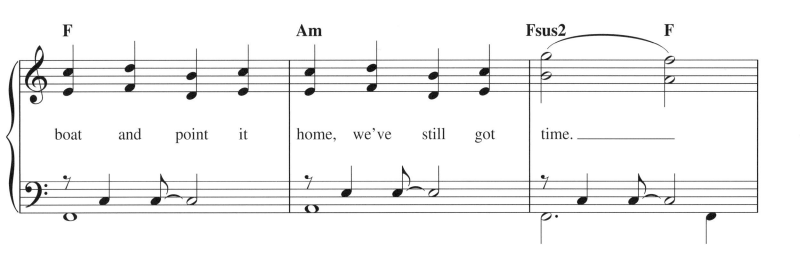

boat and point it home, we've still got time.

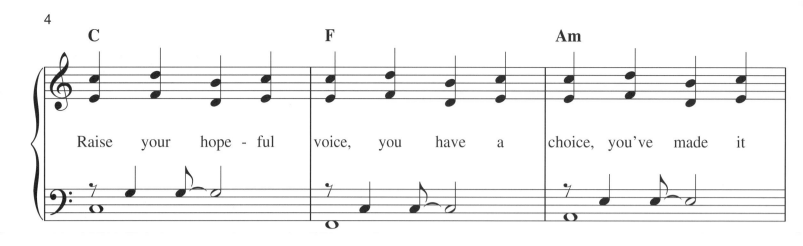

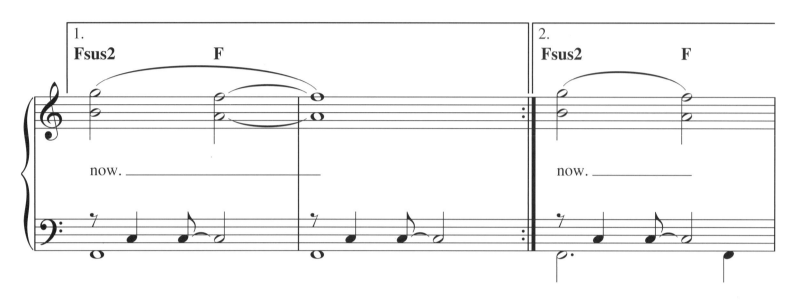

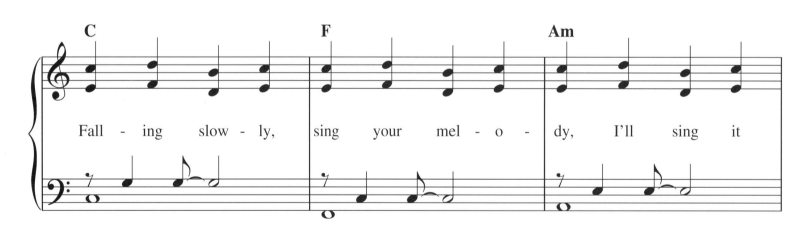

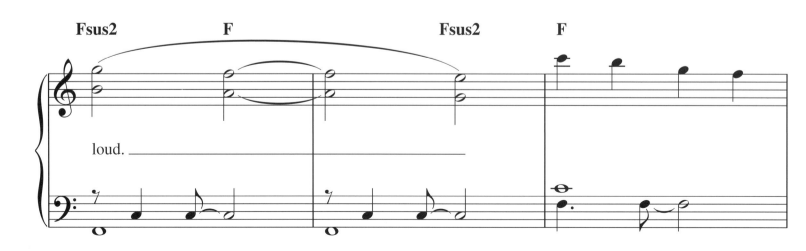

IF YOU WANT ME

Words and Music by
MARKETA IRGLOVA

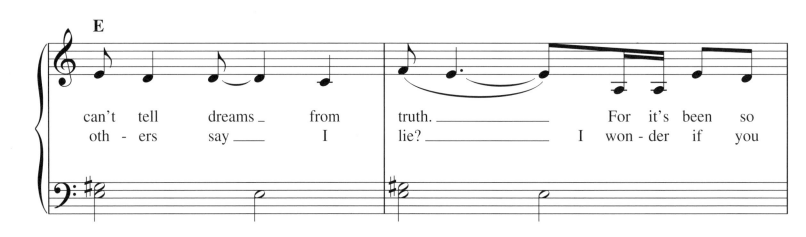

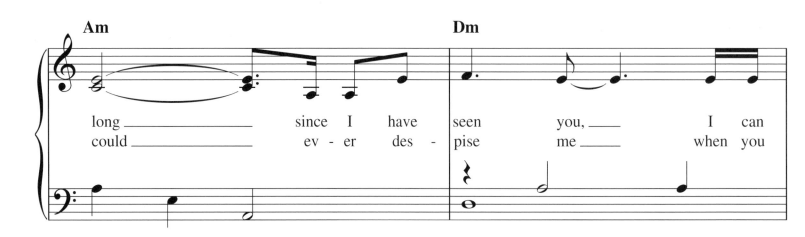

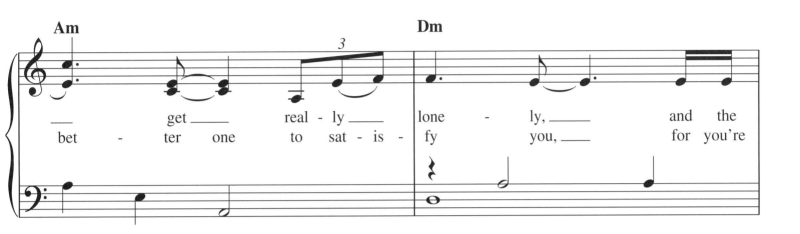

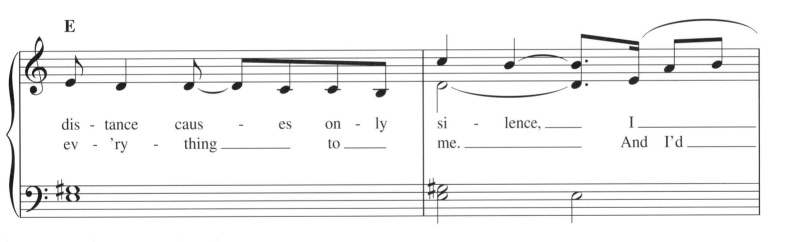

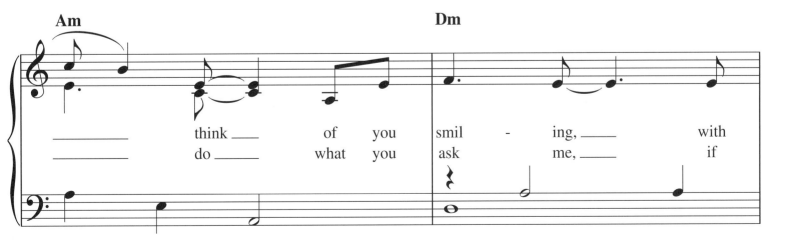

BROKEN HEARTED HOOVER FIXER SUCKER GUY

Words and Music by
GLEN HANSARD

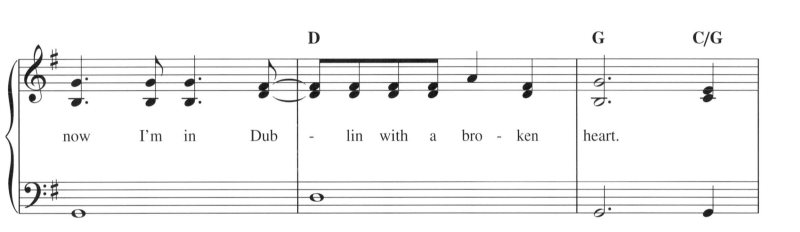

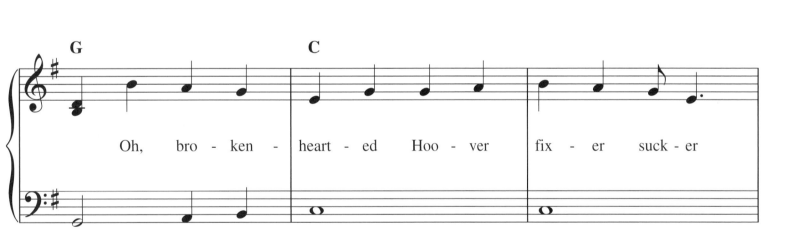

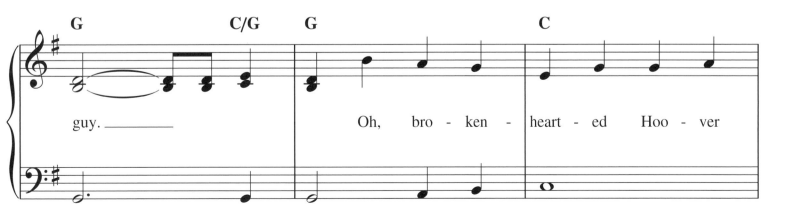

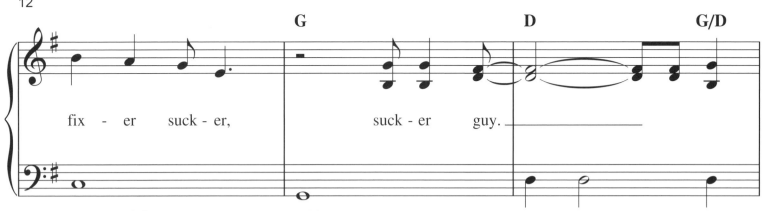

fix - er suck - er, suck - er guy. _____

One day, I'll ___ go there and _____

win her once a - gain. But un - til ___ then, I'm just a suck-

- er _____ of a guy.

WHEN YOUR MIND'S MADE UP

Words and Music by
GLEN HANSARD

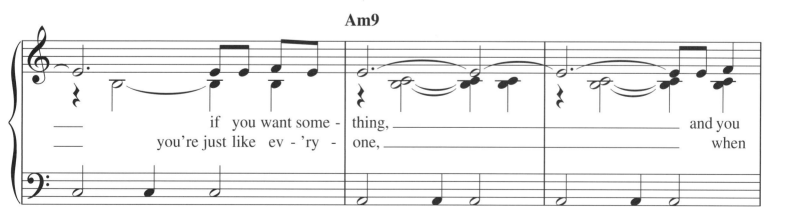

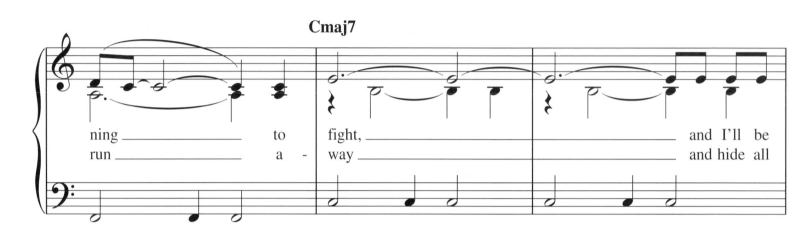

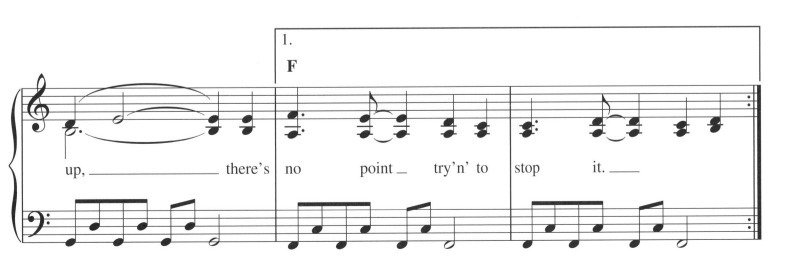

no point _ e - ven talk - ing. _ When your mind's _____ made

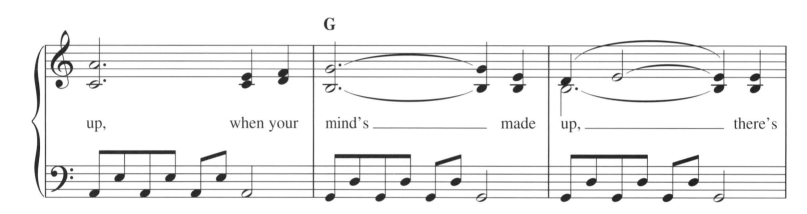

up, when your mind's _____ made up, _____ there's

no point _ try'n' to fight it. _ When your mind, _____

your mind. _____

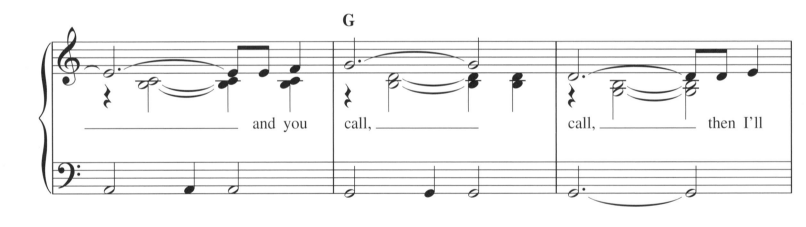

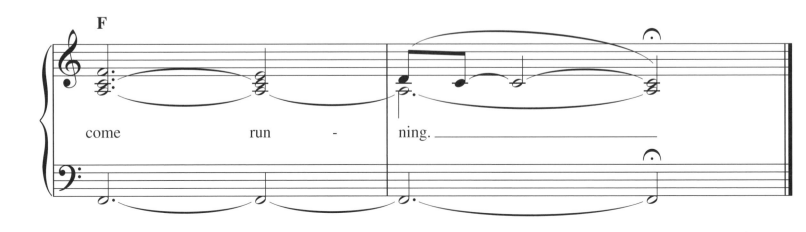

LIES

Words and Music by GLEN HANSARD
and MARKETA IRGLOVA

With pedal

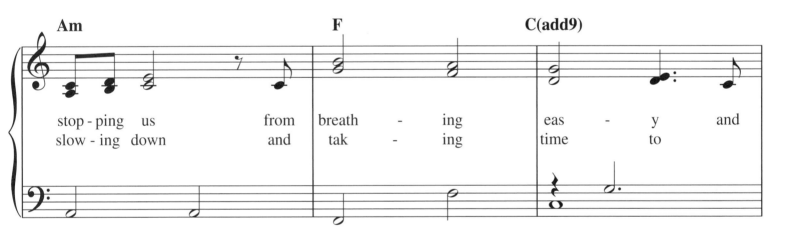

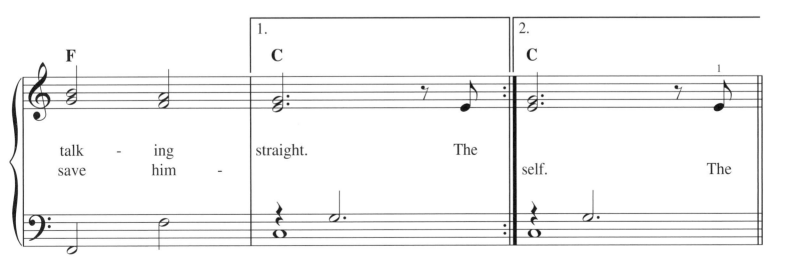

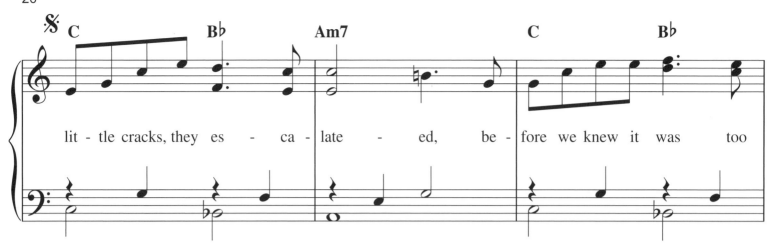

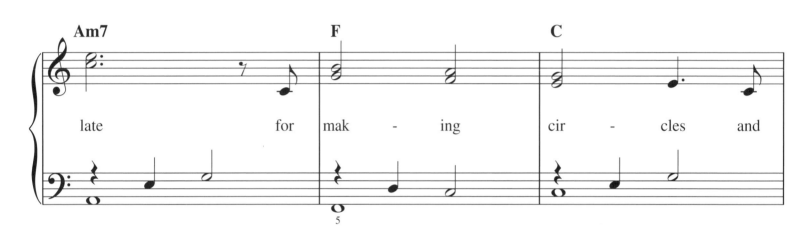

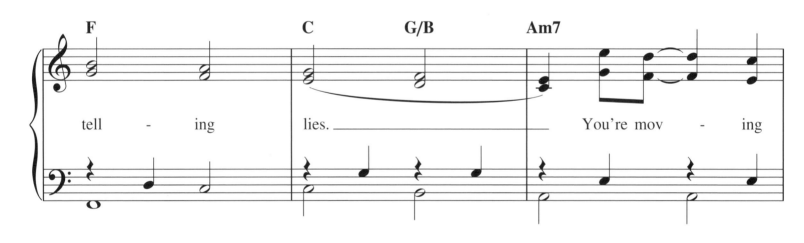

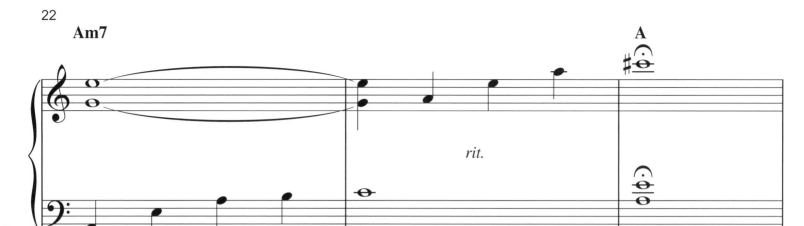

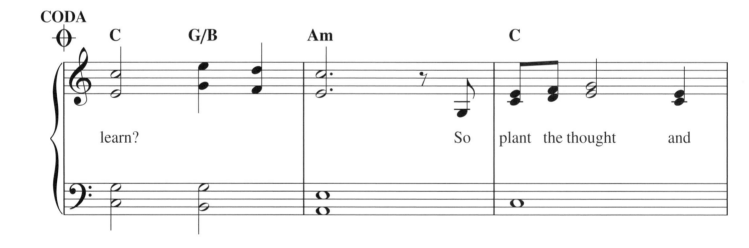

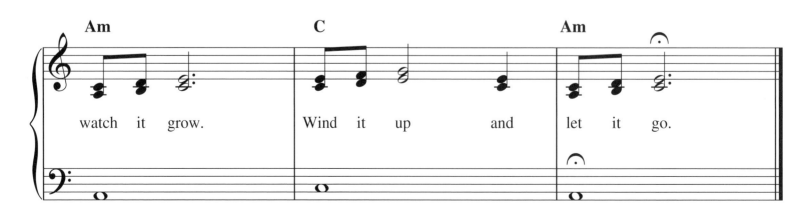

GOLD

Words and Music by
FERGUS O'FARRELL

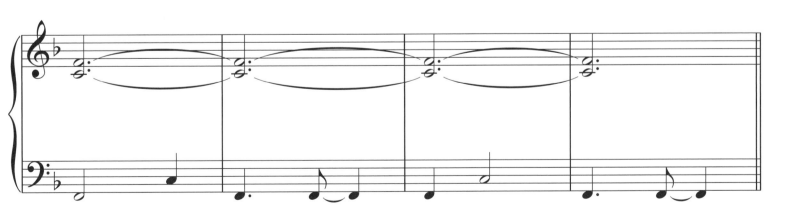

24

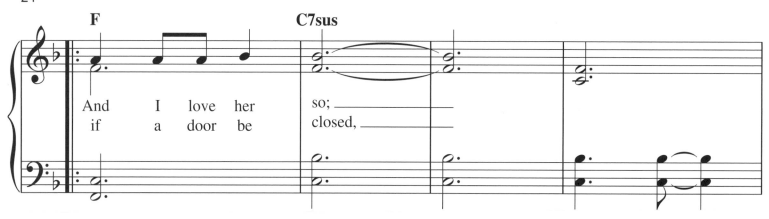

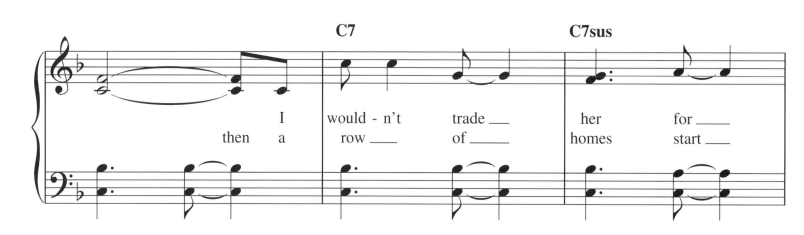

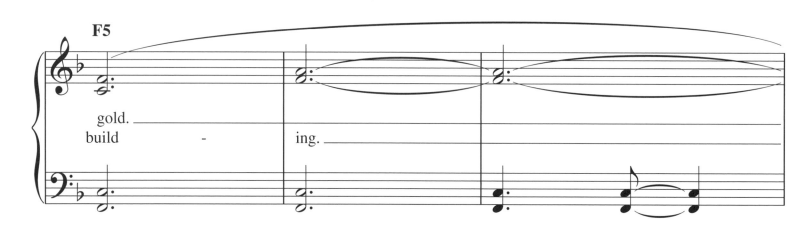

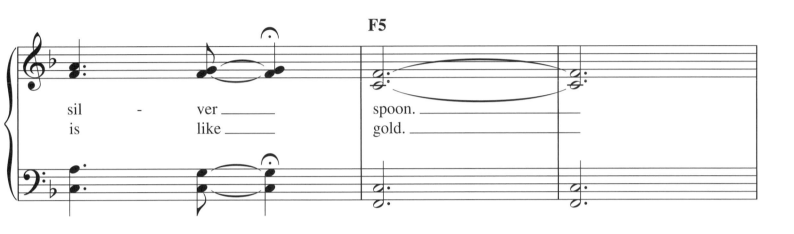

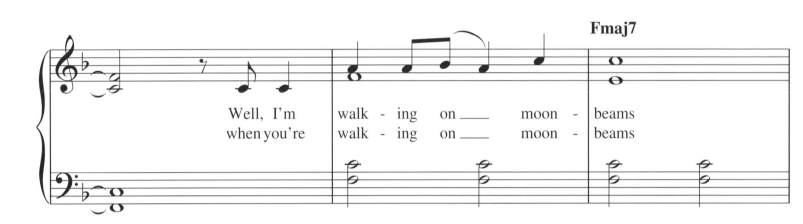

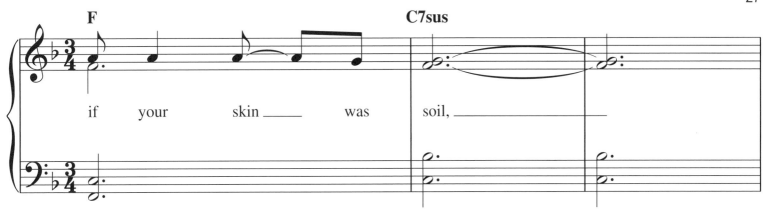

if your skin _____ was soil, _____

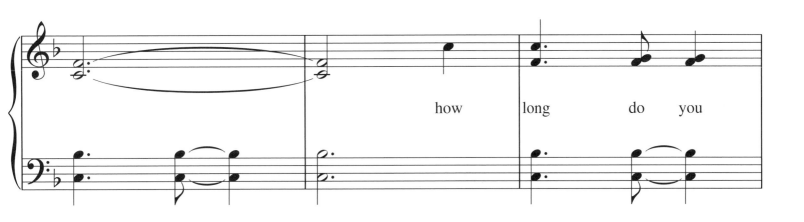

how long do you

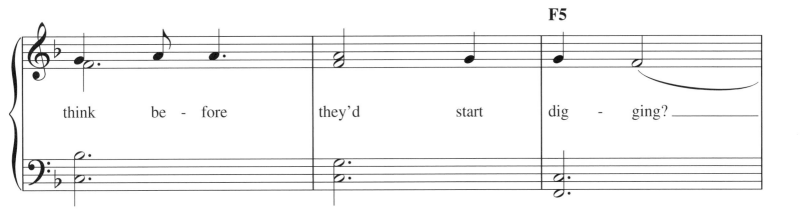

think be - fore they'd start dig - ging? _____

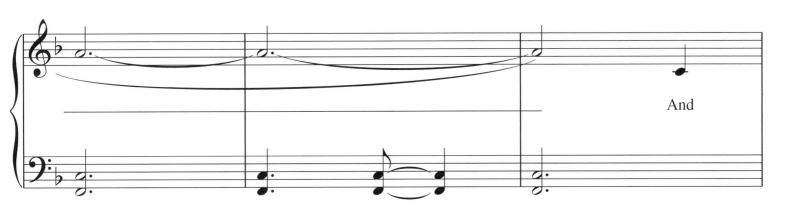

And

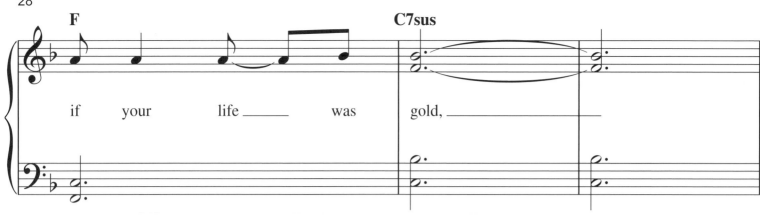

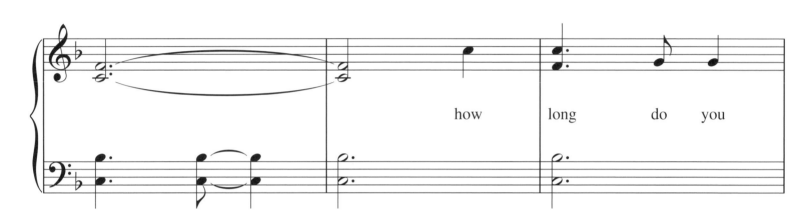

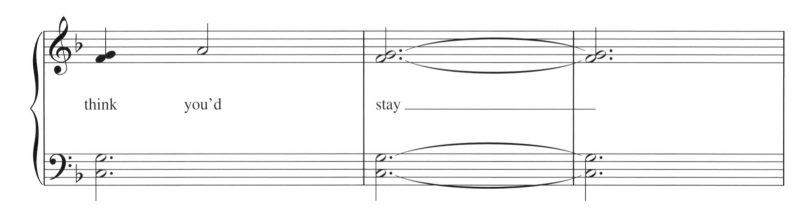

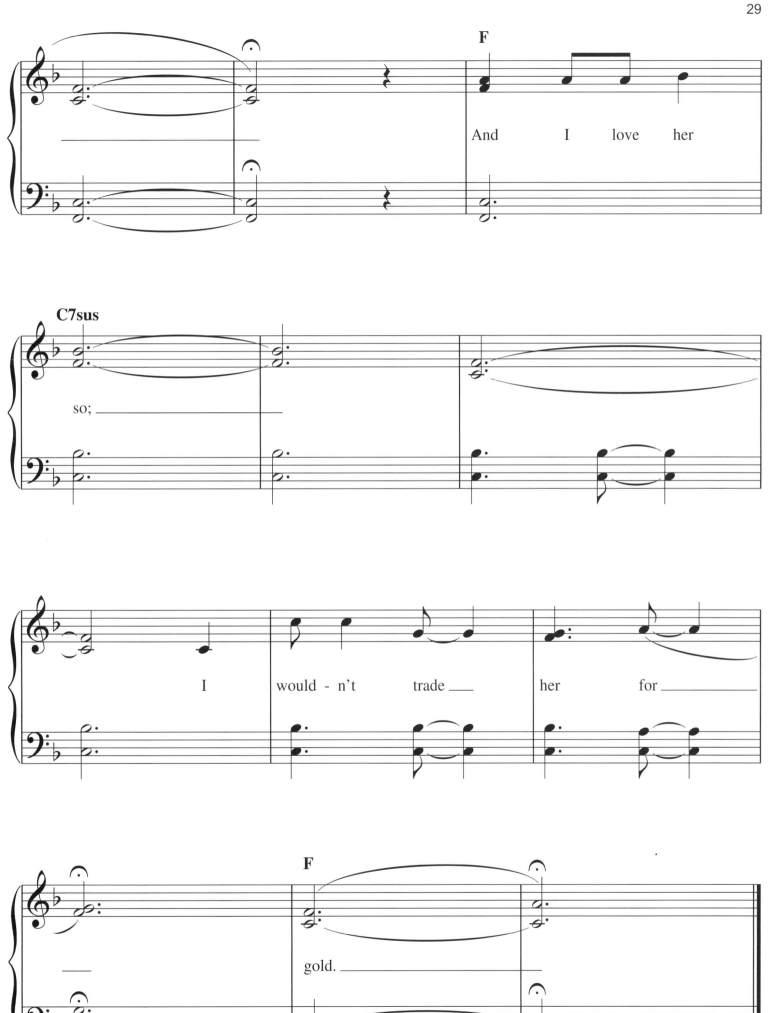

THE HILL

Words and Music by
MARKETA IRGLOVA

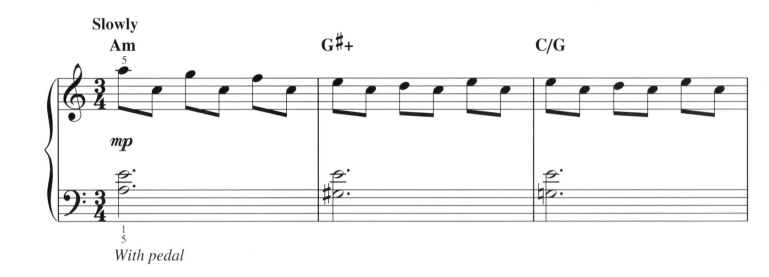

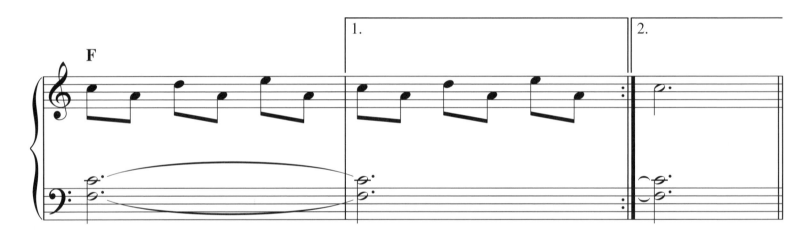

Walk - ing up a hill to - night when you have closed your
Please try to be pa - tient and know that I'm still
Look - ing at you sleep - ing, I'm with the man I

F
Am

eyes.
learn - ing.
know.

I wish I did - n't
I'm sor - ry that you
I'm sit - ting here ___

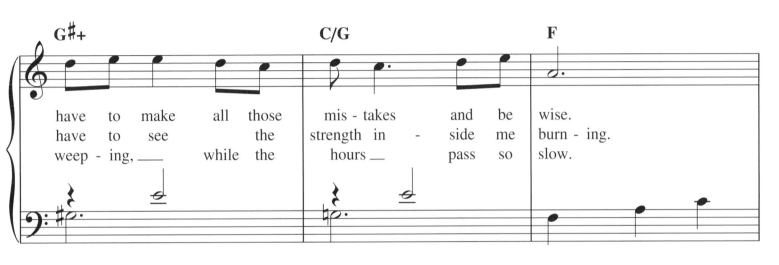

G#+
C/G
F

have to make all those
have to see the
weep - ing, ___ while the

mis - takes and be wise.
strength in - side me burn - ing.
hours ___ pass so slow.

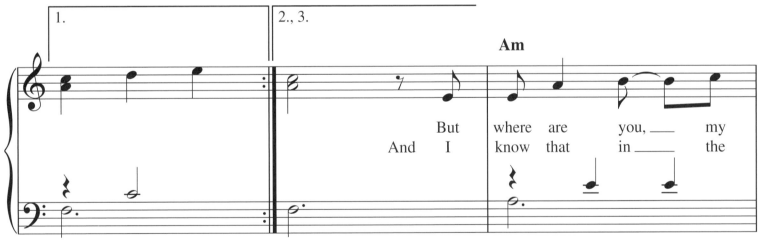

1.
2., 3.
Am

But where are you, ___ my
And I know that in ___ the

G#+
C/G
F

an - gel, now?
morn - ing, I'll

Don't you see ___ me cry - ing? ___
have to let ___ you go, ___

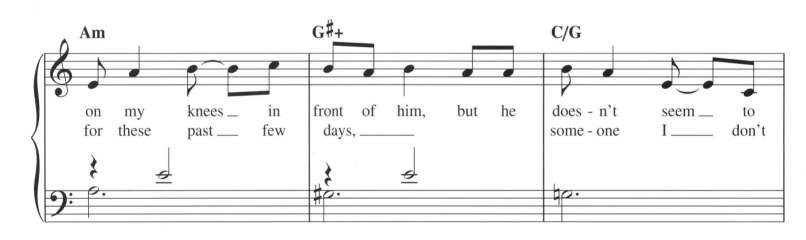

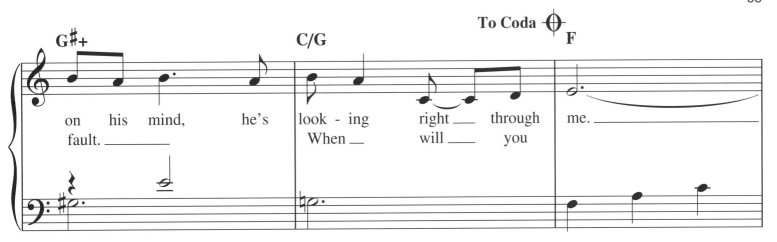

on his mind, he's look-ing right ___ through me. ___
fault. ___ When ___ will ___ you

Am I let-ting my - self down _____ be -

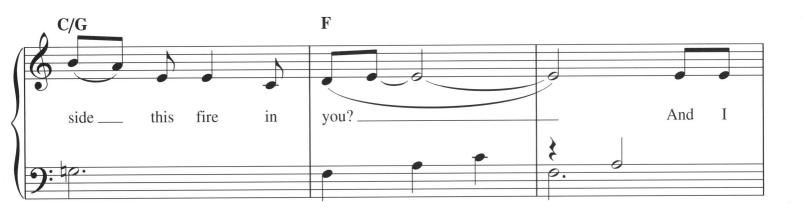

side ___ this fire in you? _____ And I

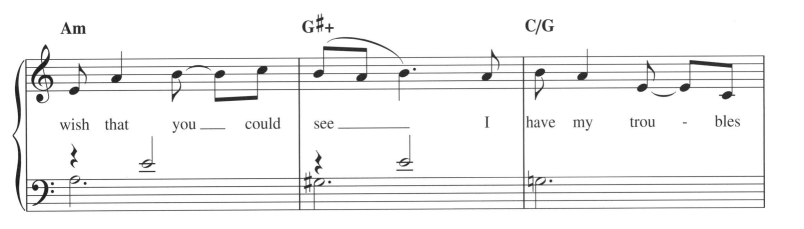

wish that you ___ could see _____ I have my trou - bles

too. _____

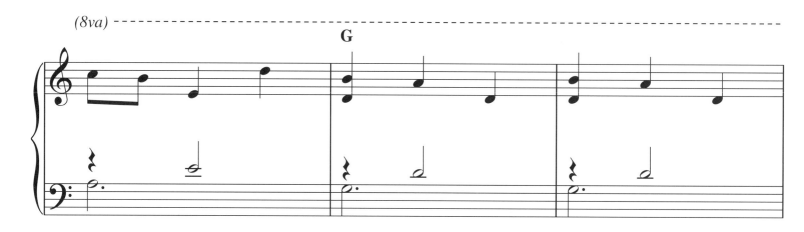

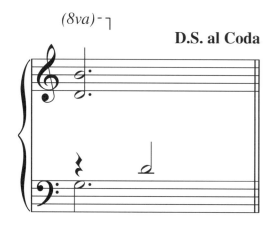

D.S. al Coda

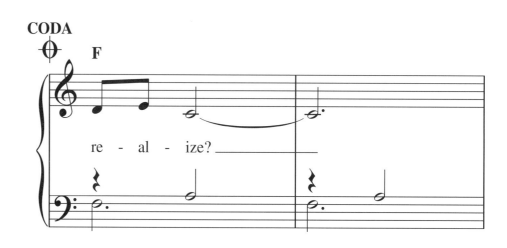

CODA

re - al - ize? _____

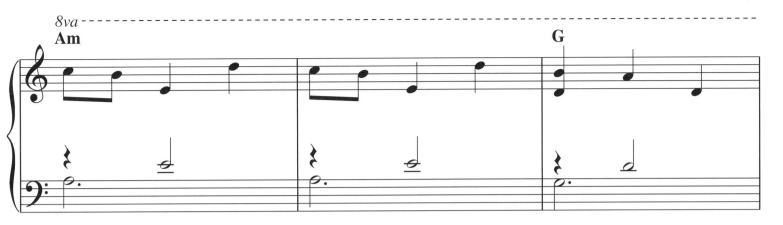

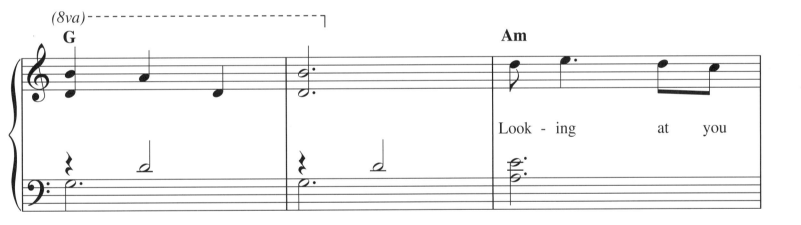

Look - ing   at   you

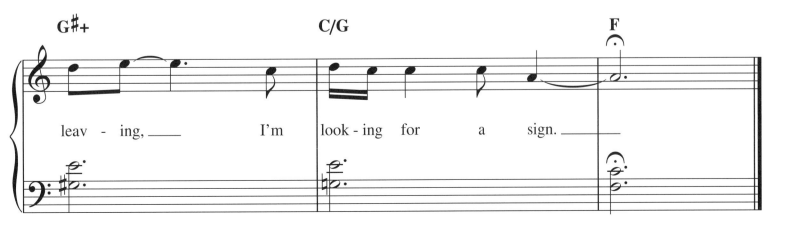

leav - ing, _____   I'm   look - ing   for   a   sign. _____

FALLEN FROM THE SKY

Words and Music by
GLEN HANSARD

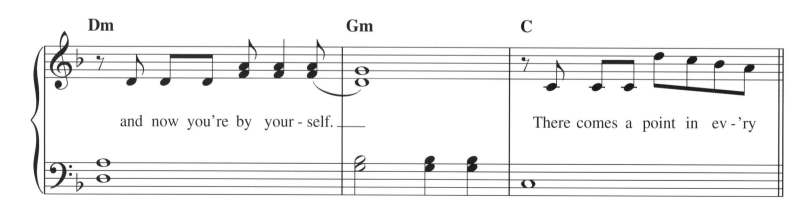

37

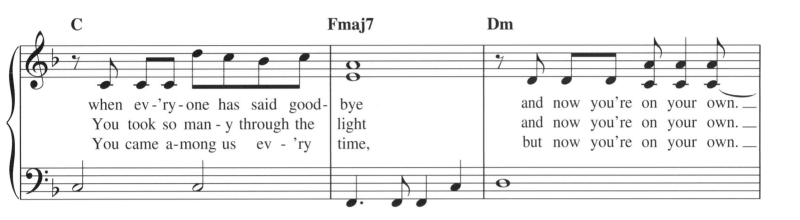

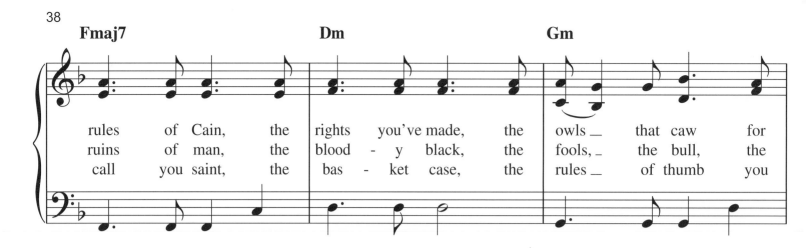

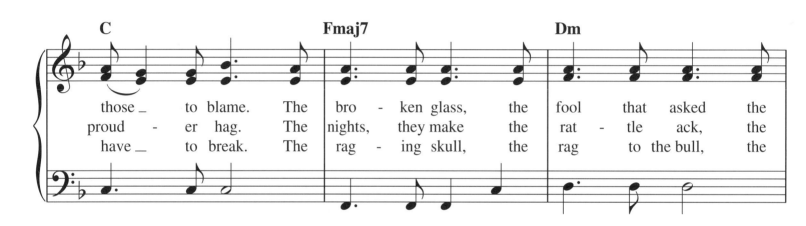

The rules that nev - er, ev - er mul - ti -

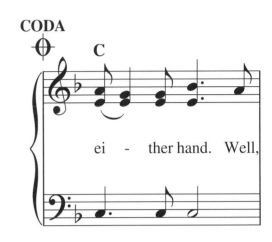

ply.   You must-'ve fall-en from the   ei - ther hand. Well,

I   will make   my   work - er that,   I   know _ this place   I

know _ this time.   *rit.*   You must-'ve fall - en from the   sky.

LEAVE

Words and Music by
GLEN HANSARD

"I can't wait for - ev - er," is all that you said
And I hope you feel bet - ter now that it's out.

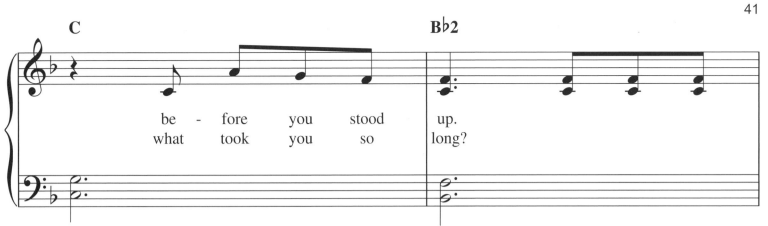

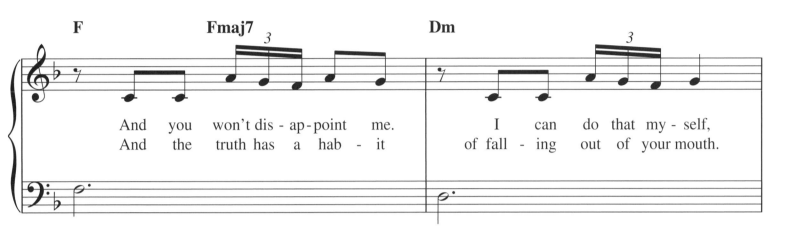

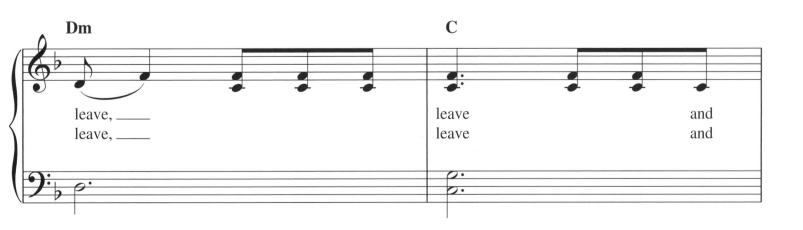

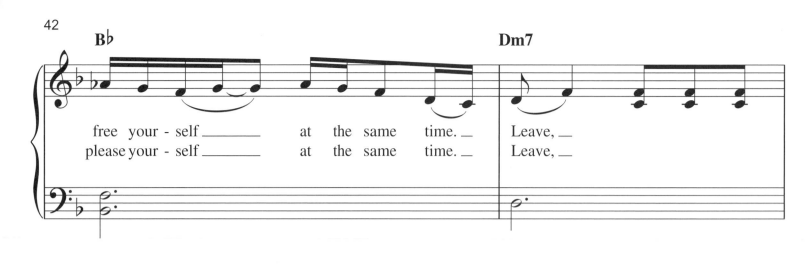

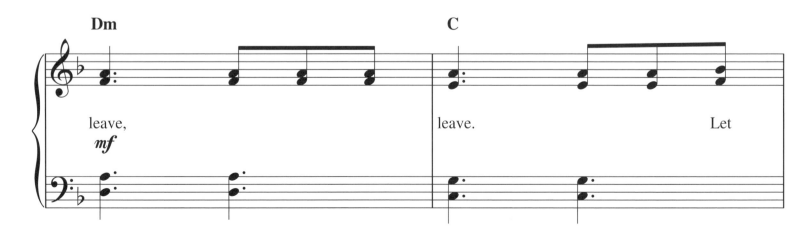

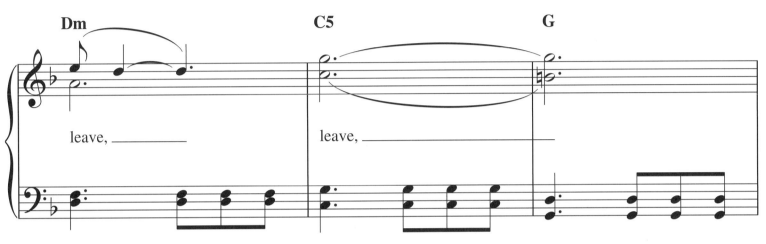

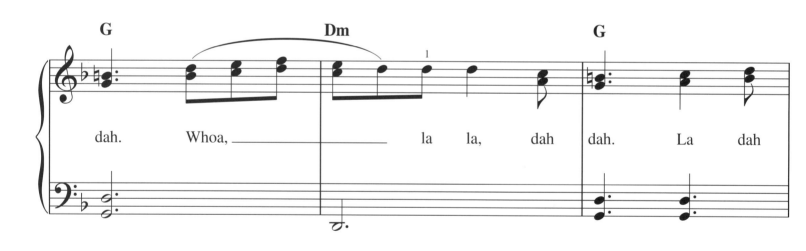

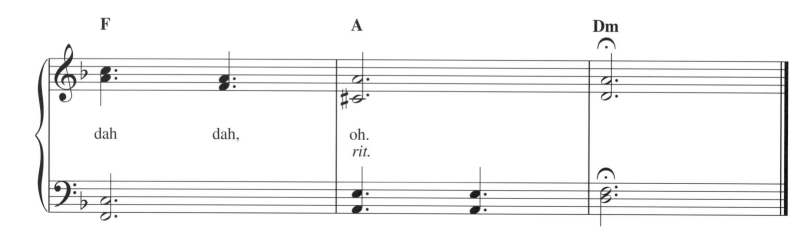

TRYING TO PULL MYSELF AWAY

Words and Music by
GLEN HANSARD

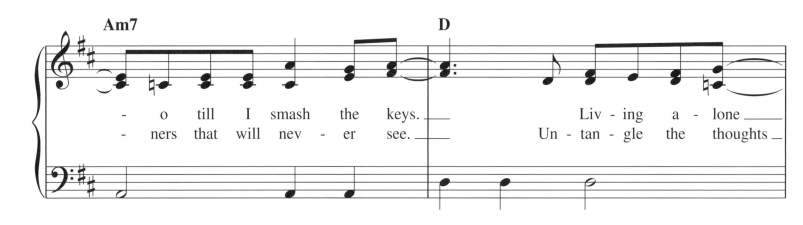

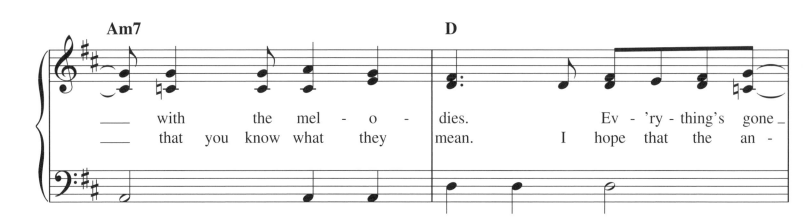

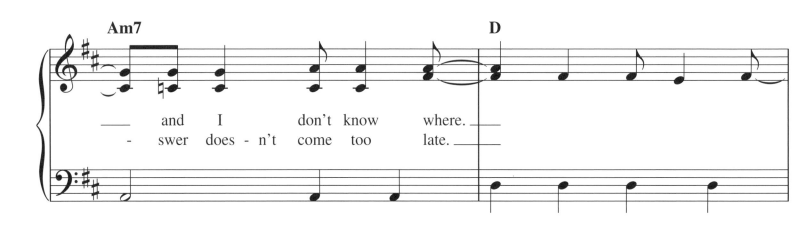

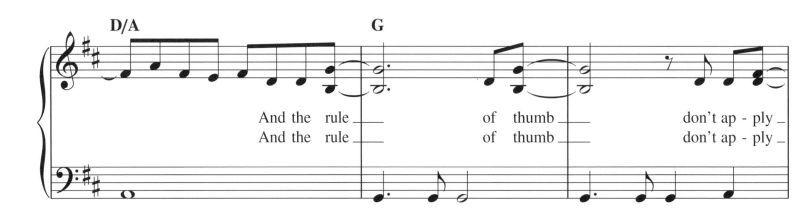

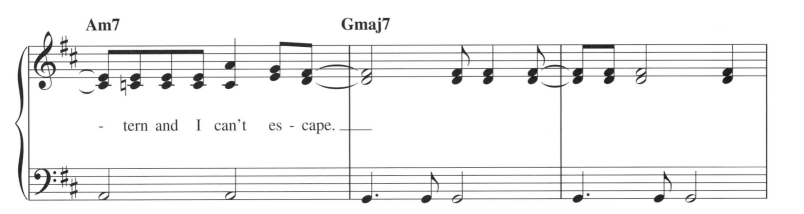

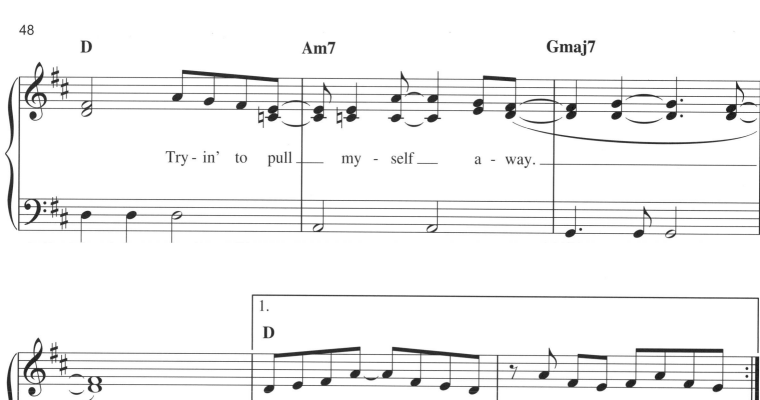

Tryin' to pull __ my - self __ a - way. __

1.

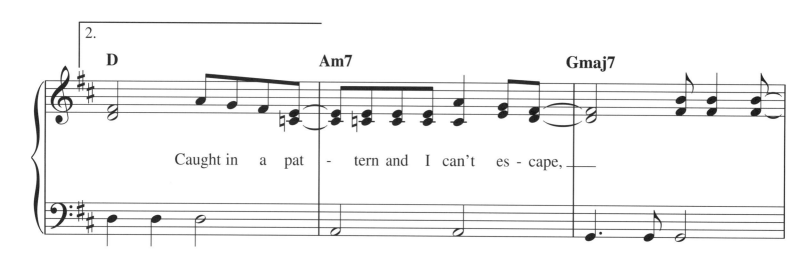

2.

Caught in a pat - tern and I can't es - cape, __

ev - 'ry-thing's gone, __ ev - 'ry - thing's gone, ev - 'ry-thing's gone. __

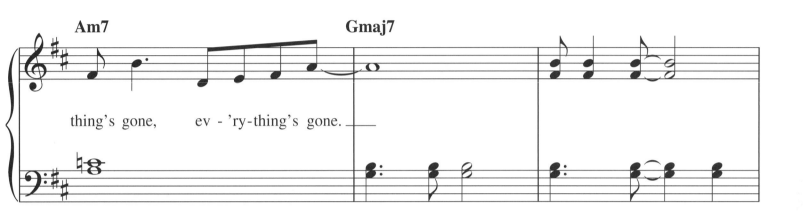

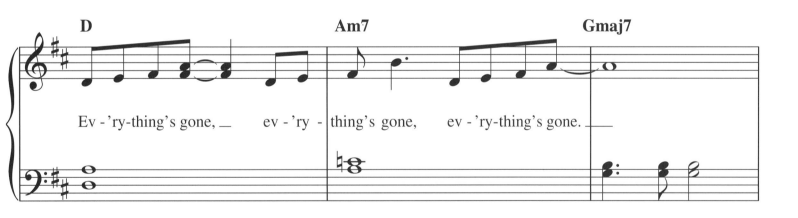

ALL THE WAY DOWN

Words and Music by
GLEN HANSARD

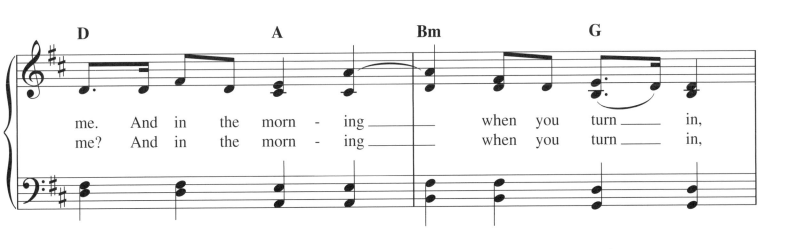

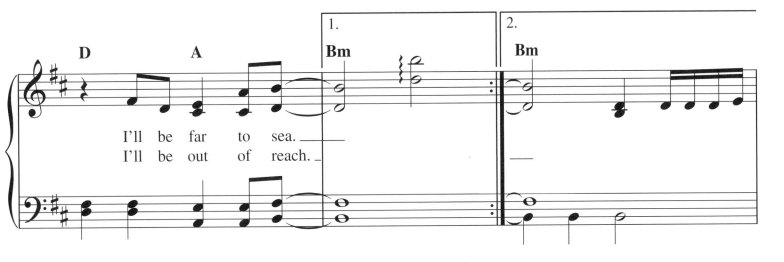

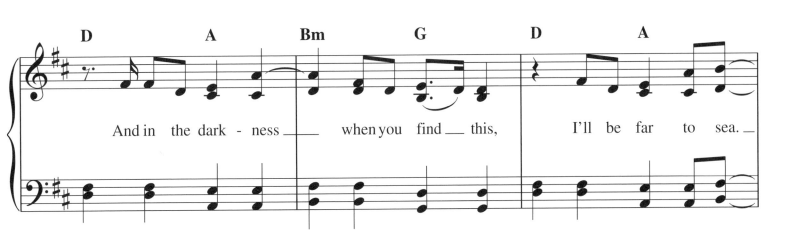

And you have bro - ken me ___

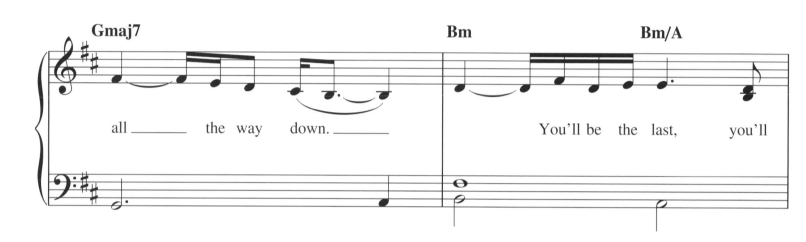

all ___ the way down. ___ You'll be the last, you'll

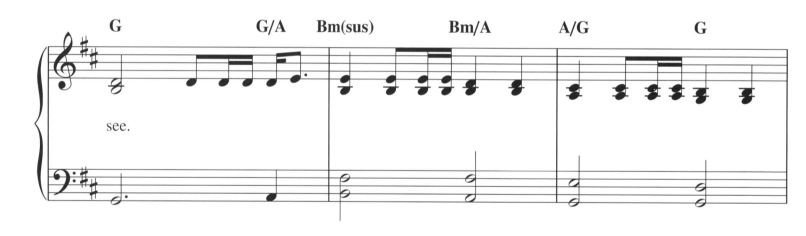

see.

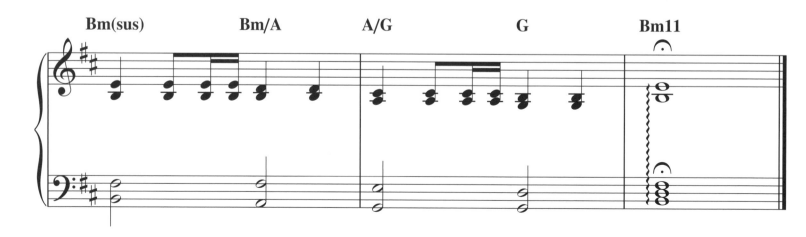

ONCE

Words and Music by
GLEN HANSARD

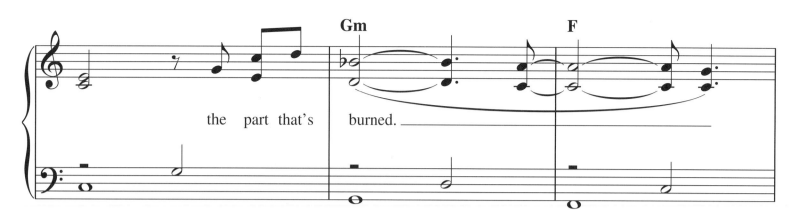

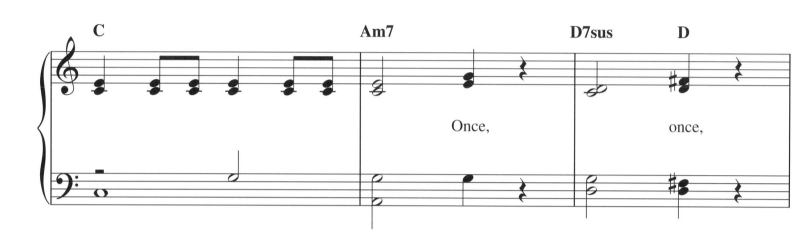

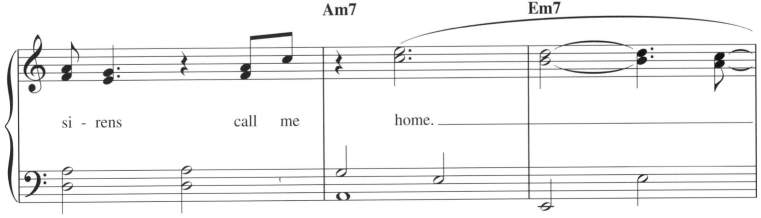

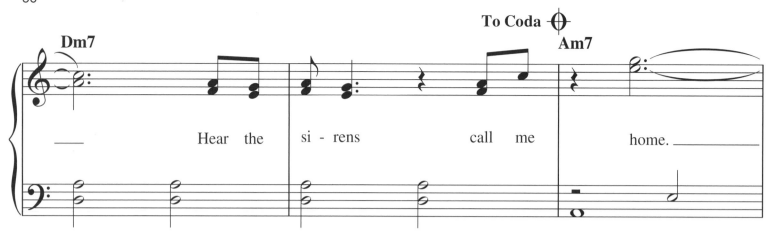

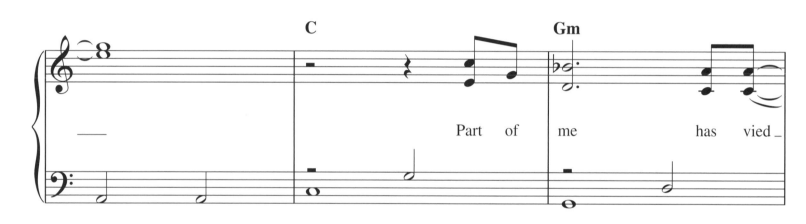

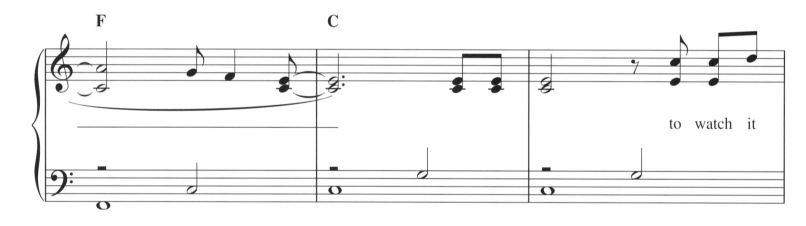

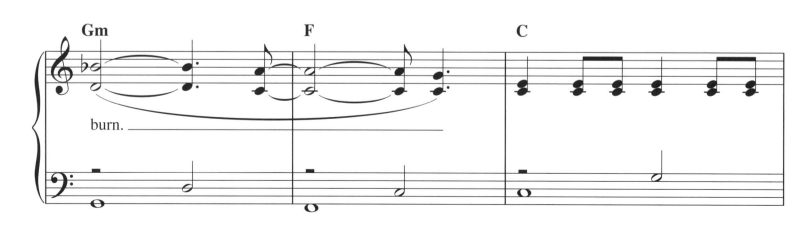

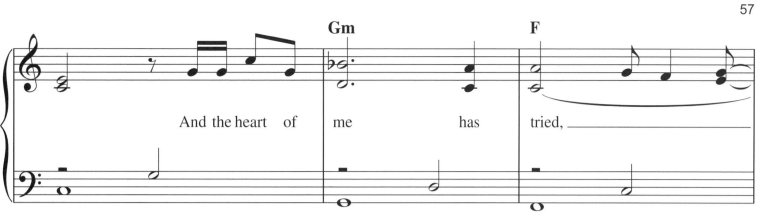

And the heart of me has tried, _____

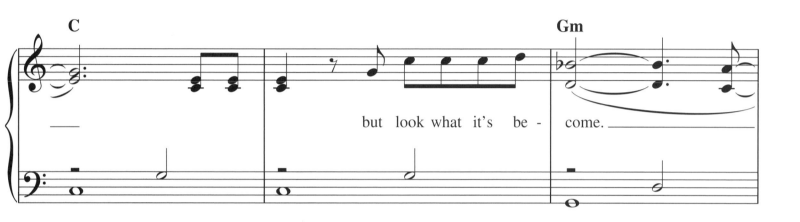

_____ but look what it's be - come. _____

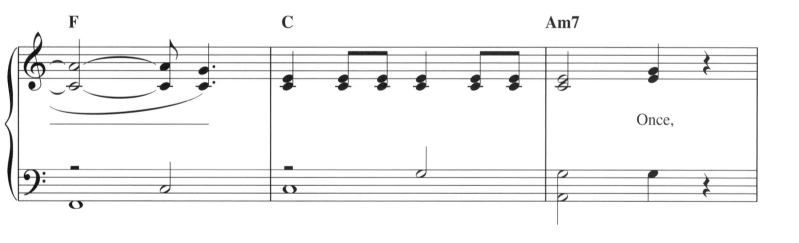

_____ Once,

once, I knew how to look for you.

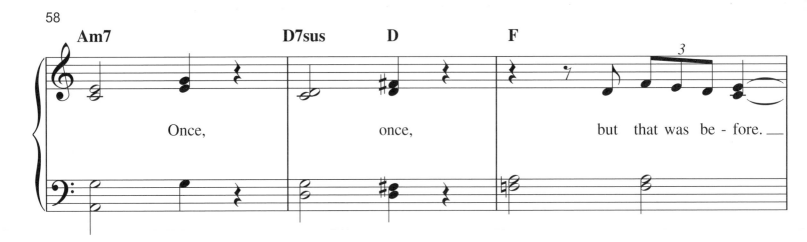

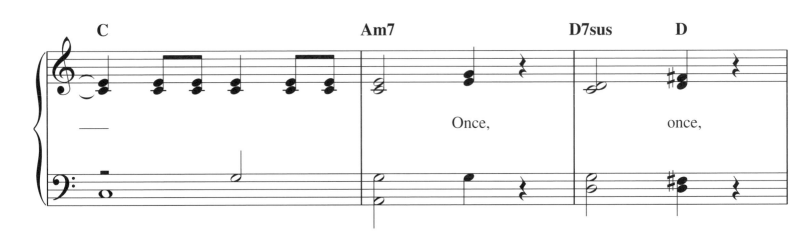

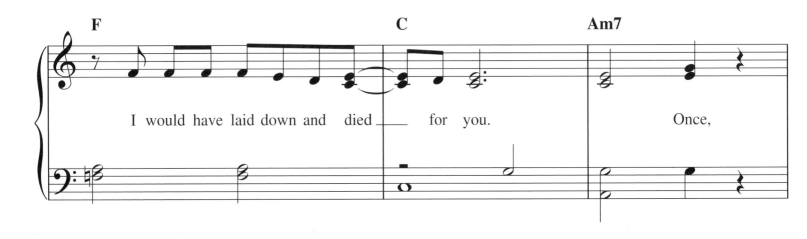

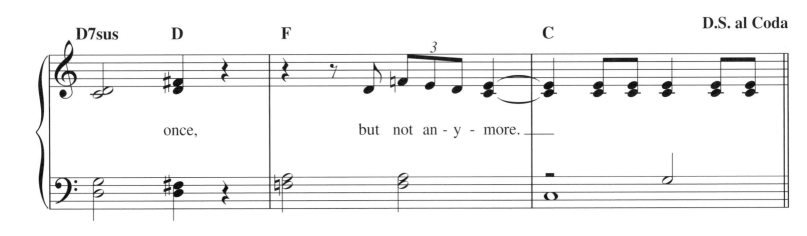

SAY IT TO ME NOW

Words and Music by GLEN HANSARD,
GRAHAM DOWNEY, PAUL BRENNAN,
NOREEN O'DONNELL, COLM MACCONIOMAIRE
and DAVID ODLUM

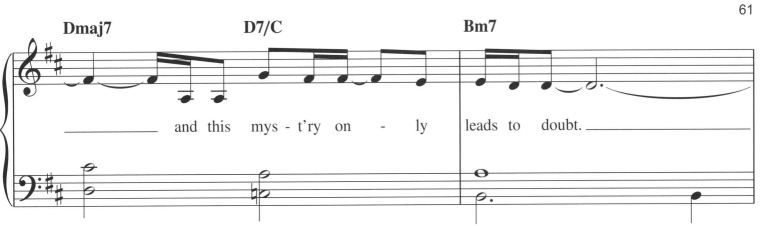

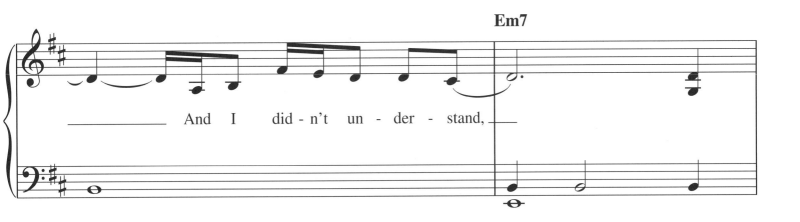

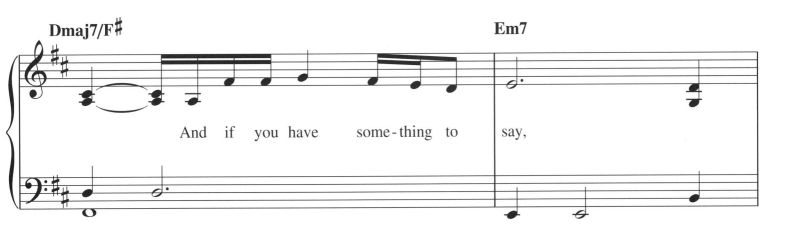

you bet - ter say it now.   'Cause this is what ___ you've

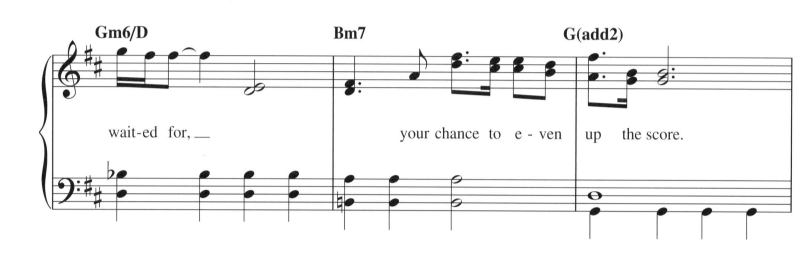

wait-ed for, ___   your chance to e - ven up the score.

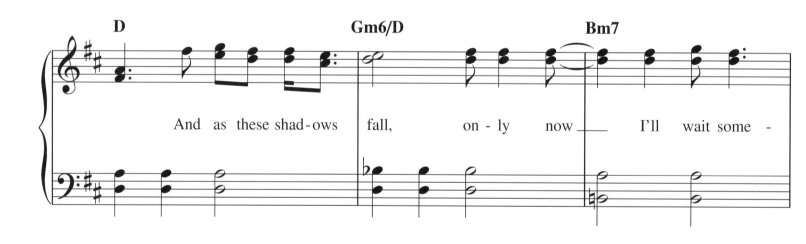

And as these shad-ows fall,   on - ly   now ___   I'll   wait some -

how,   yeah. ___   'Cause I'm pick-ing up ___ the mes - sage line,

and I'm clos - er than I've ev - er   been   be - fore.

So   if you have some - thing to say,   say it to me now.

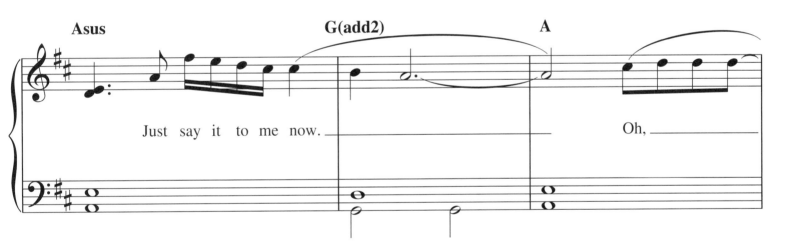

Just say it to me now.   Oh,

oh,   oh, no,   no.   *rit.*